Vacant Chairs

poems

Vacant Chairs

Linda Blagdon

Distributed by:
Engen Books
www.engenbooks.com
info@engenbooks.com

First mass market paperback printing: August 2017

Cover Image: Liz LeDrew

Table of Contents

I dedicate this book of poems to the one whose empty chair stands as a symbol of the love I had for forty-four years.

To my husband, David Stephen Blagdon, whose love and encouragement gave me the courage to share my simple poetry with you.

In my lifetime there have been a lot of vacant chairs, but I've never regretted knowing those who sat in them. The loved ones I have lost, their memories outweigh the cost of my heartache and my bitter tears. Now I will sit for a time and remember their smiles, until mine becomes the vacant chair.

DAVE

What I'd give for another day with you
But tomorrow I'd want another day that's true
There would never come an end to the days I'd want to spend
With you, my love, my husband, and my friend
Jonna, John, Cory and I,
never got a chance to say goodbye
It broke our hearts that you had to go
We miss you so much down here below
You treated every person as your friend,
though you were in pain you did not complain
I'll try to model that the best I can,
Until we are reunited once again.
Fly free with the angels up above
Give my family and friends there all my love
Tell Jesus I will serve him until my end
Goodbye my love, my husband, and my friend.

LIGHTHOUSE MEMORIES

Lying face up to the top of the lighthouse
Feeling the night breeze on my face
The stars they seem so near in a sky that's crystal clear
I remember these childhood days with peace.

I wish I could spend one more night there,
To stand atop that lighthouse once again
To hear the fog-horn blast its warnings across the waves
To feel the evening mist upon my skin.

To stand atop that lighthouse in the morning
To see the fog dissipate to the sun.
To see the flash of silver as salmon nets are hauled,
To see the boats go home when day was done.

To see the lobster pots piled in the dories,
As they slowly weave in around the shore.
To see my father wave to each boat as they passed
And to stand atop that lighthouse, just once more.

That way of life is slowly disappearing,
And I like so many hate to see it pass.
Where will our children find such tranquility and peace?
In a world that is changing much too fast.

MEMORIES OF DAD

The memories of those days and summers on Francois Western Point are very precious to me. I hold those memories close to my heart for it was there when I became aware of whom my father was. He would keep everything spotless and would bake current buns and cook sometimes to help mom. Dad took time to be with his children; helping Cyril and our cousin, Kevin to swim, take us berry picking, out in the boat and once in a while, he would take us all into Francois for a treat at the stores. I especially remember the time he brought back six pounds of green grapes and a pile of cheesies . Mom was not too impressed but Cyril, Kevin and I were. I think Liz was too young to remember but then again, I think she can remember when she was born (ha-ha).

Dad was also good at his job and many a fisherman, coming into the store where I worked, expressed to me how much they missed my father after he passed away. He would always be there on the Point waving to them when they came in from fishing. Those memories of dad, Uncle Bob hauling his salmon nets, and the fishermen hauling the lobster traps will always bring a smile to my face. I am sure that there are lots of people who can identify with these memories. Growing up on a light station and living in small isolated communities are the things that wonderful stories are made of.

LIFE ON THE SEA

The winds up to Southered, it's straight in the bay.
The boats have come in with their catch for the day.
But one boat is missing; it's getting real late.
We'll have to go searching; the men they debate.

The women are gathering into the store,
The men are nervously pacing the wharf.
Storm clouds are gathering, it soon will be dark.
Something has happened is all they remark.

The wives are at home trying to be calm.
The children have gathered, there's some in her arms.
Will dad be getting home later today?
"I hope so my babies," she's heard to say.

She pictures his boat as it bobs on the waves.
She prays his won't be a watery grave.
Like so many fishermen, who's gone there before,
Never to leave that old ocean floor.

The big boats are out searching, a call has come in.
Somewhere up shore they've spotted the men.
Much later the story is told over and over
How frightened they were when their boat caught afire.

How they swan for their lives and battled the waves,
Trying not to succumb to a watery grave.
There's not too many who fish for their bread
Hasn't felt that very same dread.

The harbors' all thankful that they are home again,
Fishing for a living is what they have claimed.
The sea it can be a friend or a foe
But life on the sea is what they all know.

HOME

Colors are blended with the water; shadows are reflected.
Day loses itself to the night; moon rises uninhibited.
My troubles ease in the gentle breeze,
This night should go on forever.

The boats are now reflected in dark moonlit waters.
All the chores are done; outside no one wanders.
Most of the household sleeps; I lie awake.
Tomorrow I'll be leaving.

Melancholy-- happiness and sadness thrown together.
This place confining and yet enriching, will my leaving be forever?
I never know why, but my heart gives a sigh,
Every time from here I'm departing.

Each time I come to this harbor, I wonder is it my last.
Some how our present and future are all tied in with the past.
Francois is itched in my memory; this place has given and taken.
My heartstrings are wrapped around these hills,
Until my last breath is given.

TREPASSY TO FRANCOIS

Oh, the boats are coming in, the first is Henry Greene.
We haven't seen our daddies in a while,
They've been gone for months to put food in our mouths.
That's the way it was when I was a child.

The next around the point is Freeman Dollimount
His boat is called The Parachute.
We see the children run, to gather on the wharf
That's the way it was when I was a child.

Coming around the point I see a flash of green
I'm the happiest child that you have ever seen.
My dad is home again, if only for awhile,
That's the way it was when I was a child.

Women hollering to each other, "The boats are home again".
They all gather, to welcome back their men.
Laughter, smiles, and tears, they've put away their fears.
That's the way it was when I was a child.

Green duffle bags to carry home, bake apples in a jar
You know you won't have to carry them too far.
For the homes of fishermen were close to a stage and wharf
That's the way it was when I was a child.

Lodge meetings they now attend, soup suppers at the hall
And on the table you'll surely see a bottle of alcohol.
Their laughter it would ring as old songs they did sing.
That's the way it was when I was a child.

From Trepassy to Francois, they've journeyed home again
Thank God they are safely home once more.
A few more weeks and again they'll leave this shore.
That's the way it was when I was a child.

FISHING ON THE FOAM

When I was a little boy upon my mommy's knee,
I would watch the boats from home as they went out to sea
I fell in love with things they did and all their different ways
That's why I'm a fisherman until my dying day

I joined a fishing trawler, my father's boat was she
I was just fifteen years when I went out to sea
My mother prayed to God above, "Please bring him home"
I never wanted my little boy to work upon the foam

Now my fishing days are over, the government says no more
You have to sell your licence and work upon the shore
My mom is in her ninety's and yet she said hooray
I never wanted my little boy to sail upon the spray

Now, once in a while, I take my boat to the deep blue sea
For there on the water is where I want to be
When I leave this life and God calls me home
I know once more He'll want me to sail upon the foam

FREEDOM

Our soldiers are over in Afghanistan
They are in that terrible place
We think of their faces in childhood
With memories that none can replace

They grew up in quaint little places
Could look and see boats on the sea
Now they look at the sands of Kandahar
And wonder what's beneath their feet

From Ramea, Burgeo, and Francois
Harbour Breton and McCallum they came
And also from cities like St. John's
To serve in this never ending game

We place a white rose on their coffin
The last post on the bagpipes we hear
We pray it won't be one of our family
But it's sad someones child is lying there

Our children grew up in communities
That were wholesome, happy, and free
Now they fight so other children
Can enjoy school and their liberty

We pray to our God in heaven
To end the war and the strife
But somehow deep in our hearts
We think this struggle is for life

Yes, our children are over in Afghanistan
Their lives, Lord, in Your hands we place
Let us not harbour thoughts about who's wrong
But pray for Your love and grace

DAMASCUS ROAD

Have you ever walked a Damascus Road?
Have you ever carried a heavy load?
Was your life filled with sin and your heart full of pain?
I walked that road once, but never again.

The life I was living was only for gain,
It offered no peace; it gave a lot of pain.
Now the riches I strive for are friendship and love,
Since I felt my Savior's hand, touch me from above.

For I met my Savior one lonely day,
He answered my prayers and He took my sin away.
He called me His child and promised His love,
I felt His peace flowing down from above.

When you lay your sins down at Jesus' feet,
You should be prepared His spirit to meet.
Your sins will be gone and your soul will be light,
And your eyes will appear as given new sight.

Life only lasts for a short while on Earth,
And death it is nothing but a second birth.
Ask in Jesus name and you will receive,
For we will all be raised, if we only believe.

For I met my Savior one special day,
Now I ask for guidance as I journey on my way.
I want for others this Peace and Love,
Found through the Spirit, sent from above.

MEMORIES OF FRANCOIS

My memories go back when I was a girl
The village of Francois was my only world
Some of my family and friends they are gone
But the longing for past days are still very strong

I remember Brother Jack and John Henry his friend
Cutting up ice for a few cents to spend
And lighting the fire up at the old school
Always talking of a joke they could pull

Riley, more serious, but yet full of glee
Would send us to borrow and we'd charge him a fee
He'd pay me a dime to keep my hair long
And then torment me all the day long

I'll never forget my sweet brother, Ralph
Especially the last days in his failing health
His smile it would greet us as we walked through the door
Those memories will linger for ever I'm sure

Cyril, the quiet one, with a heart as good as gold
Didn't know a lie, when to him it was told
I love him so dearly, God only knows
But a can that I threw almost cut off his nose

Liz was a Christmas gift from God up above
Our family so proud, we wrapped her in love
She drove us half crazy with her off the wall views
But a finer sister I never could choose

Jimmie and Dora I can not recall
They made up our family eight children in all
We'll be all together some day by and by
In that great home above where no one will die

Mom and Dad are among the best
For more than once they were put to the test
The faith they had and the love they have shown
Give us good values, now that we're grown

I now have to mention my grandmother, my friend
Many an hour with her I did spend
She read from the Bible to my cousin and me
What we didn't understand, she taught us to see

The old house of ours down by the sea
Play a main part of those fond memories
Nin, Uncle Charlie, Lizer, and Gram
Mable, Lydia and dear Jimmy Sam

Sunday morning at our house was a rowdy ole time
Jimmy Rich and Roy Durnford for a hair cut would come
Rita would drop in to borrow or Uncle Bob for a talk
Then mom would send us youngsters out for a walk

Then after dinner, the house cleaned and swept
Uncle Gord's crowd would visit, we'd tear the place up
When we met together, I'll never understand
Why we don't carry around the print of mom's hand

Those high hills of Francois keep calling to me
The valley below and the calm of the sea
The brook that runs so fierce in spring
The church bells on Sunday so lovely would ring

I have to conclude for this is too long
But the memories I have, could go on and on
Like Nancy and I over to Uncle Nar's
Or under the bridge, "Oh, those beautiful stars"

All who read this, I know you will see
That my home, friends, and family mean Heaven to me
No matter where I travel, no place on this Earth
Can compare to Francois, the home of my birth

INTO THE LIGHT OF DAY

When life's road is ended and death has surely come,
Do you wonder if God will take you home?
Won't you ask for mercy and guidance on your way?
All through the darkness into the light of day.

What a promise He has given; don't you let Him down,
So come to the Savior today.
Put your hand in His and you'll walk in peace,
From darkness, into the light of day.

If you think you're not worthy, don't hesitate to ask
For no one is perfect, free from sin.
Jesus took it on Himself to wash away all guilt
And when life is over, He will surely let us in.

God sent His precious son to die upon the cross
So you and I could be truly free.
If we ask forgiveness, heaven won't be lost,
Cause Jesus died for us on a cross at Calvary.

GOD'S PROMISE

He painted the rainbow across the blue sky,
And gave us a promise that never will die.
When troubles like rain come, just look to the sky,
Lift up your heart to your Father on high.

Mountain top feelings come once in a while,
They will sustain you through many a trial.
Don't let your doubts in, just close your eyes
And picture His rainbow across the blue skies.

Please don't forget what He did long ago,
He gave Noah a promise and I tell you so.
That promise not broken still comes in the sky,
There's hope in the Heavens from our Father on high.

He painted the rainbow across the blue sky,
And gave us a promise that never will die.
The great arch of beauty still comes in the sky,
The colors all chosen by our Father on high.

I AM , I AM

I am, I am the God of Jacob and of Abraham,
The Babe who was born in Bethlehem.
I am the Son of God, I am, I am
I am the stars, the moon, the sun, I am, I am
The sea when it's rough or calm, I am
The One who gave you life, I am, I am
I am Father, Son, and Spirit, yes I am.

I am, I am the burning bush that Moses saw, I am
The guide who lead you to the Promised Land
And paid the price for all, I am, I am
I am the One who bids you come to Me, I am
The road to your salvation, yes, I am
The One who can give eternal life, I am
I am the Savior of this world, I am, I am.

I am, I am the Shepherd of my sheep, I am
And yes I was that sacrificial lamb,
Who died on the cross for you, I am, I am
I am the way, the truth, the life, I am
The descendant of David's line, I am.
I came down to Earth to walk with mortal man.
I am the Son of God, I am, I am.

I am, I am the You in me and me in You, I am
I can be the Shepherd or the Lamb
The presence, love, and conscience, yes I am
I am a child of God, I am, I am.

WHY ? (Sept. 11, 2001)

We made love that morning, the first time since her birth.
I wanted you to stay, but off you rushed to work.
I see your smile so happy, as you left us there alone.
I know you would not have gone, if only you had known.

I try not to remember the sirens, lights, and noise.
I try to remember happier times, that would've been your choice.
I know that you look down on us, from the heavens above.
I hope that you are happy there, where all are clothed in love.

Here on earth I struggle to find comfort in our child.
I wish you could have lingered to see her tender smile.
She took her first step today, and I asked God to let me know,
If you could see her and in some way show me so.

A rainbow suddenly appeared across the bright blue sky.
I know that is my answer; I'll no longer question WHY?

THE TRUE VINE

You are the true vine and we are the branch
You love us so much; You keep us attached.
All of life's good gifts, they spring forth from You,
Peace, joy, life, and a love that is true.

On the heart of a green tree, for our sins You died,
The branches forsaken, for three days they cried.
Then as the true vine, You rose again,
Like evergreen branches, forever to reign.

Now You live in us, if we'll live in You,
When we feel like we're swaying, we can go to the root.
To the deepest foundation this world can find,
We are the branches and You the true vine.

NATURE'S GIFTS

Clouds are but little frowns, sunshine is God's smile.
Rain is His blessing to refresh us for a while.
The Stars at night are His laughter,
As he looks at us from above,
And the beautiful colored rainbow
Is His great promise of love.
The thunder and lightning are His passion
That stirs something deep in our souls
And His blanket of forgiveness,
Is white like the winter's first snow.
The howling wind sometimes must be His broken heart cry,
When he looks down on us in sadness
And says, "For their sins I died?"
He sends green grass each spring to remind us,
That through Him we can be renewed,
Lovely like the summer's first roses,
And fresh like the morning's sweet dew.
The last days on earth are like Autumn,
With each leave that falls from the tree,
The years rush off so quickly,
Each color a sweet memory.
Look to the earth and to nature,
God you surely will find,
This earth and all the planets
Are not from the hands of mankind.
Our God is awesome and wonderful,
His praise everyday we should sing,
We are a part of His planning,
Our God made every good thing.

VACANT CHAIRS

All the doors in town say welcome friends but no one comes around.
They sit there in the rocking chairs; in their homes there's not a sound.
The children they have all grown up and gone their separate ways
And now they long for company in those last lonely days.

I know dear parents you must think we don't really care,
For if we did we'd try to find   time to visit here
Time seems so rushed dear mom and dad we've children of our own.
I guess we'll feel the same way when our children they have grown.

Take a little time if you can to phone them up and say
That you thought about them as you worked away the day
And each night when you kneel down to say your evening prayer
You ask God to protect them; watch over them with care.

For a day will come too quickly when they're no longer here
We'll all be sad and hurting when we see those vacant chairs.
But Fathers' Day and Mothers' Day will come with no regret
If you tell them now you love them and treat them with respect.

LIGHT OF HOPE

The unexpected became the expected

The breakdown became the new building up

The wreckage became the new foundation

The day that began as darkness became the Light of Hope

The unexpected visitor lifted me to that place

Where once again, I knew You protected me

The question: Who am I?

Found the answer

A Child of God

BLESSED HEM OF JESUS
(Based on Luke, Ch. 8)

For years and years I've suffered; life seems so unfair.
Sometimes I sit and wonder if anyone really cares.
They say the man named Jesus is coming down our road,
I feel if I could touch Him, He'd heal and make me whole.

The crowds are pressing in on me, so rough on every side.
"I know this is my only hope", something inside me cried.
My hand fell on His blessed hem; I knew that I was healed.
He said "Someone has touched me." Then a man beside me yelled.

What can I do? I have to speak and tell what has been done.
So, nervously, I went before the Blessed Holy One.
Standing trembling before Him, my story I did tell.
He said, "Go in peace, my daughter, your faith has made you well.

Go in peace my children and tell what has been done,
For only then can others be brought unto the Son.
We have to tell of peace and grace and all its healing powers.
For when we touch the hem of Christ, these gifts can all be ours.

SWEET PEACE

Tears have often fallen
like rain
When we miss my loved
ones when I am in
pain
when we turn to Jesus
and in his word abide
there's peace sweet
peace on the other side

Troubles make us stronger
that's often hard to see
challanges come daily is how it
sometimes seems to be
when our thoughts turn to
Jesus, Father forgive them he
cried, there's peace sweet peace
on the other side

There's peace sweet peace on the other
side. Though i have my problems
His love we cannot deny
when we see a rainbow, his
promise in the sky
There's peace sweet peace
from the other side.

LAYREADERS' CONFERENCE

Your very being is filled with anticipation
Friday as you travel, Mint Brook your destination.
You hold back a little as you approach the dining room door
Wondering, hoping, praying to greet friends you've met before.

What a joyful reunion at the chapel Friday night
The service free and open; the Lord shines forth His light.
We go back to our cabins in wonder and thoughts so deep
Tired from our journey but we very rarely sleep.

Saturday brings forth teachings that we eagerly digest
The instructors really show that Christ is the special guest.
The walls so bare and special; so humble the wooden floors
Peace that passes understanding is found beyond these chapel doors.

Sunday morning after breakfast, heaviness lies in our hearts
We've gotten to know each other a little more but now we have to part.
We pray that God will bless us as to our homes we go,
Inspired by each and everyone our hearts with love aglow.

MY SILENT FRIEND

Sunlight dancing through my window today, reminded me of You,
Then later You were there again when I spied a tiny bloom,
And once again, I saw You as a little child at play.
Thank you, God; my silent friend is with me here today.

Silent, yet your voice speaks volumes as You reach inside and touch,
The vulnerability of my soul I try to hide so much.
You always bring a smile, a tear, "they are a part of You".
Use me as you want to Lord and let Your love shine through.

Sometimes it seems You are stubborn and You will not let me hear.
I search to try and find You, but you've seemed to disappear,
But when my darkest moment comes, I feel your gentle hand,
Like a robin in the springtime, You show Your greatest plan.

Yes, Your silence brings renewal, that's what I've certainly found.
You carry me through my weakest points when I am feeling down.
When darkness is all around, You show the path to take,
My silent friend, You add so much like icing on the cake.

A PRICE HE HAD TO PAY

How I miss your golden hair and your pretty eyes of blue
And I miss the colors that you used to wear.
If I could only turn back time, when those happy days were mine.
If I'd known, I'd never gone to war.

We really didn't have to go to war in Vietnam
And forever I will feel a sense of shame.
The United States will always pay for mistakes they made that day,
And my sight is the price I had to pay.

I cannot see my little girl, but I feel her tiny face
And I try to draw a picture in my mind.
I know her hair is blond and her little legs are strong,
And you say her eyes are just like mine.

A white cane is now what people see
And they think that I helped to keep them free.
The government was wrong; I was forced to go along,
I wish instead I'd gone to Canada.

No I cannot look into my baby's eyes
And sometimes late at night it makes me cry.
The war has left its mark; I'm forever in the dark
But each soldier had a price he had to pay.

WORLD PEACE

I climbed up Jacob's ladder tonight and plucked a tiny star.
And as I pressed it to my heart, I prayed, "Put an end to war."
The Heavenly Hosts all came and sang, "Peace to all mankind."
Listening to their song of peace, this hymn came to mind.

O God of love, O King of peace,
Make wars throughout the world to cease.
The wraths of sinful man restrain,
Give peace, O God, give peace again

If everyone on Earth tonight would sincerely sing this hymn,
I know that all the wars would cease and peace would reign again.
Send Your Holy Spirit to touch each troubled soul,
Then love would fill our very lives and You could reign below.

WORLD HUNGER

Tonight across the sea there's someone hungry
I sit here with my table full of food.
I wonder if the little money sent there
Is spent on them or really does much good.

Someday they'll have a banquet up in Heaven
For those who've never had a feast below.
Permit me, Lord, to serve at that table
And see those precious faces all aglow.

Yes, they're out on the street so cold and hungry
For food and love, they haven't had enough.
Those helpless ones will find a special setting
In that banquet hall where all are served in love.

PARKINSON'S NORTHERN LIGHTS

Northern Lights impatiently interfere
Beyond anything to crash the planet's peace.
Beautiful but haunted,
They never seem to wait or stay in time,
Or need pursued desire,
But go on much like tonight.
Certainly, our nervous system is
Awakened and near breaking.
In the sky floats fire and curves.
The watcher strives for safety and
Longs to touch the Heavens
To restore calm.
In the chaos, Peace, sweet Peace, is found.

ONE SOUL

I know my life won't be in vain, if I bring one soul to God,
And tell him of my Savior's life and where His feet have trod.
To tell him of Good Friday, how on the cross He cried,
"Father, please forgive them," He pardoned us and died.
Then on Easter Sunday morning, He victorious rose again,
And promised us eternal life if faithful we remain.

THE CROSS

The greatest gift I ever knew was given on Christmas morn,
When God himself made manifest and Jesus Christ was born.
He came here to redeem the world but was rejected by His own.
For us who believe and haven't seen, His Spirit He makes known.

The hands that guide me daily have been abused and torn.
Each time we take His name in vain, He feels the nails once more.
On His head there should have been a halo or a crown,
Instead we placed a headpiece made out of cruel thorns.

Yet He loved us so very much, He from the cross did cry,
"Father please forgive them", gave up His life and died.
The veil that separated Heaven and Earth, that day was torn in two,
The sacrifice He made that day was made for me and you.

Yes, the hands that guides us daily, were nailed to a rugged cross,
If we were treated fairly, our lives would have been lost.
But the love He has for each of us, this world cannot explain,
So we wear His cross now proudly, to show we are redeemed.

THE SUN

The Sun rising every morning without words seems to say
I am sent here as a present to brighten up your day.
To put a smile upon your face; to encourage the birds to sing
To show you the rolling plains and clear blue mountain streams.
To help remind however dark the night,
God created me to slowly rise to gently show the light.

My setting is quite different; people sometimes stop in wonder
To marvel at my colors as I quickly pass down under,
A mountain or horizon, I am taken from your sight
To rise again on another shore, where day precedes the night.
To brighten up the universe; to chase away the fear,
Just like my Creator, I am always here.

BE CAREFUL HOW YOU PRAY

Be careful what you pray for, it might really get done.
God has a sense of humor; He likes a little fun.
My friend wanted a certain birdhouse,
She talked about it everywhere she went.
While doing her laundry one morning,
She discovered six baby birds in her dryer vent.
She called me up and told me,
I laughed and said in fun,
"Be careful what you pray for,
It really might get done."
The birds they stayed for about a month,
She didn't turn the dryer on.
For that month, I tell you, birds were Annie's song.

The morning light always hurt my eyes,
So Dave rushed out to buy a blind.
He bought the blind a real dark color,
And hung two blinds on top of each other.
We rented an apartment; the curtains were all in place,
But when we moved the following week,
The windows were all fake.
We didn't have a window; the curtains were only for show.
Be careful what you pray for,
God's humor you might get to know.
For weeks I had prayed my room was dark
So the sun wouldn't hurt my eyes.
God played on me a little trick and made me realize,
He is not always serious; He likes a bit of fun,
Be careful what you pray for; it really might get done.

HOUSEWIFE'S LAMENT

I wish I had a week to myself,
To live in my home with nobody else.
No one to clean for,
For no one to cook,
No one to even come in and look,
At the dust or the clutter on furniture and shelves
Oh, I wish I had a week to myself.

I'd wear what I wanted,
Sleep as long as I could,
Read all day long and not worry about food.
To ask for a week would really take nerve,
After thirty years together,
I think I deserve.
It may be selfish and I may be a geek,
But I would really like,
To live alone for a week.

HUSBAND'S RESPONSE TO WIFE'S LAMENT
By: Dave Blagdon

Because the seed has been planted,
Your wish can and will be granted.
You shall have a week to yourself,
To live in our home with nobody else.
Only yourself to clean for,
And for yourself to cook,
No one will bother or come in and look.
There's not much dust on furniture and shelves,
You can certainly have a week to yourself.

Wear what you want,
Sleep as long as you can,
Read all day long; don't worry about this man.
To ask for a week is really not so bad
After thirty years together, I think it's not mad.
I think you deserve it; not selfish or a geek,
But Cory and I are granting this week.
We will go camping when the weather is fine,
Fishing, boating, and some good quality time.

JIMMY SAM'S RAM

Jimmy Sam he had a ram
The damnest ram had Jimmy Sam.
He caught me down by our house
I ran frightened like a mouse.
Over Walt Andrew's steps I did fly
Screaming Mary, oh I'm gonna die!
I fell in through her open door
And dropped half dead upon the floor.
As much as I liked dear Jimmy Sam
I sure did hate his damn old ram.

MY GREY HAIR

When I was young my hair was black
And hung in curls down my back.
I know that no one paid much heed
To the color of hair upon my head.

Now that I've been turning grey
It's advice I get most every day.
"Dye your hair, don't wear it long
You'll look much younger" is their song.

It's funny I tell them that now they care
About the color of my hair.
If I was a man they would all say,
"He looks distinguished turning grey".

I gave in once to try their dye,
The results I got would make you cry.
My hair it turned a pinkish red
"Not dark enough" was all they said.

Just a few weeks and I could see
My hair was turning a sickly green.
Hell with advice is what I say
I'm keeping my hair a lovely grey!

KARMA

Do you believe in karma is asked
a lot these days
Karma is a bitch is anouther
modern phrase
don't do nothing wrong, don't have
anything in your past
because karma is going to get
you and bite you in the ass
I thought a lot about karma
and I've come to this conclusion
when we talk of karma, we
leave ourselves out of the equation.
If I stole a stick of
gum and on it I did choke
everyone would say that's karma
and karma's not a joke
leave it up to karma for she'll
come back to you
do not sin anymore for you know
what she will do
karma must be the devil's wife
for sure she isn't christan
before we judge anyone else
put ourselves in the equation

AUNT ETHEL'S DREAM

The silliest dream I've ever heard
Was one of a very bashful bird
A chicken on a roaster floor
Stood and looked through the oven door
And said to the lady standing there
"Put curtains up to your oven, dear
So I'll not feel naked standing here."

ASH WEDNESDAY

Why is this morning taking so long?
Another few hours, we will be up on the pond.
This is Ash Wednesday and a Francois tradition
To take the afternoon off from reading and writing.

Yesterday was soft Tuesday, we ate pancakes galore,
Fried up in pork-fat or butter for sure.
Today is Ash Wednesday and we'll eat the fish
With no pork or butter touching our lips.

Ash Wednesday is the first day of Lent,
The afternoon on the pond it is spent,
Unless it's raining and we're kept in school
When this happens, we're a hard bunch to rule.

Today the sun shines brightly; we're a happy lot
For the afternoon off we surely got.
Run home for a minute for mittens and sleigh
Grab a biscuit or pork-bun, and we're on our way.

The hills are all covered with thick crusty snow
Couldn't be better if we ordered it so.
The snow sparkles like diamonds from the sun going down
It's another happy Ash Wednesday in our little town.

BONFIRE NIGHT

The eighth commandment we always adhered,
Until on the calendar this date did appear.
November the fifth which meant a bonfire tonight,
We'd go out and steal whatever was in sight.

Pickets that needed some nailing on,
Early next morning, they would be gone.
A wood-house and a few chunks of wood,
We'd take it all, if we possibly could.

A dragger in the harbor would also fall prey,
To us thieves on bonfire night, don't stand in our way.
Just before the fire would go out,
Rubber tires would be thrown in without a doubt.

Each year the fire would burn brighter than last,
And the flankers would often set fire the grass.
Your face would be burning from the warmth of the fire,
But you'd have to turn round to warm up your rear.

Every few minutes you'd hear someone say,
That's my ladder or birch broom gone by the way.
We all had a hell of a grin,
When someone's hen house would be thrown in.

Guy Fawkes is the man we have to blame,
For giving us all a chance at this game.
If it wasn't his hand in a very bad act,
We would have missed out on a very good prank.

ANSWERED PRAYER

She had a feeling he would soon go
And leave her alone for places unknown.
His drinking was worse and he'd sit all alone,
Not finding any comfort in family or home.

She took down the bible that he used to read,
And inside the cover wrote, "I'm missing you, Steve.
If you ever read this and you're still all alone,
Steve, I still love you, please come back home."

Years passed and the children went on their way,
To jobs and to college but she still prayed each day.
God if he's living, please let him know,
Show him what I wrote so long ago.

One evening while having a meal all alone,
A knock and the footsteps for which she had longed.
Her eyes filled with tears as she gazed on his face,
A now reformed husband stood in his place.

He'd read the bible and thought of the loss;
His wife and his children, the drinking had caused.
The words she had written showed how deep she cared.
Thank God tonight; He had answered her prayer.

MY BABY GIRL

Jonna, my baby girl,
So sweet so brown,
Eyes that squinted
Instead of being round.
You looked a little foreign
So tiny and so frail,
I looked on you and loved you
And know I always will.

I was afraid, dear daughter,
If I could really cope.
I knew not if we could give you,
The very best of homes.
I was so young and you so new,
I only wanted the best for you.

Dad and I together
Did the best that we could do.
I feel our love has often
Helped to see you through.
If you ever have a child, my sweet,
Your possessions aren't enough.
The only thing that will matter
Is if you give them your love.

OUR PRECIOUS SON

God gave us a special son to protect and to love
A beautiful blessing sent down from above
A child who would never grow old in his mind
Would remain young and carefree until the end of his time

A child who taught us to live worry free
This precious son we named Cory
A child with Downs is what they say
He brightened our lives in a spectacular way

He has given his love to me and his father
To Jonna, his sister, he's been quite a brother
A blessing to give thanks for when our journey's run
Thank you, God, for our precious son

GRAM

To me you were the kindest soul
That I have ever known.
You read to me when I was small
And cared for me when grown.
I knew that I could count on you
No matter what I'd do,
Your prayer way I've come to love
It has always seen me through.
I miss you Gram, I always will
But on my heart your love's instilled.
Your gentle smile I still can see
Gram, you meant the world to me.

GRAM'S PRAYER

Now I wake to see the light
God has kept me through the night
Keep me safe Dear lord I pray
guide and guard me through the day
may my sins be all forgiven,
bless the ones I love so well.
Take me when I die to heaven,
happy there with thee to dwell.

CHRISTMAS MORNING

Christmas morning so long ago,
A crackling fire and loads of snow,
New woolen socks and pullovers too,
Some small toys, but these were few.
Our noses were cold but our hearts were warm.
When we greeted each other on Christmas morn.
No new sound tracks or racing cars,
No beanie babies or vcr's.
Life seemed happy and stresses few
In that old fashioned Christmas that we once knew.
As Christmas dawns another year,
We hold our friends and family in prayer.
The times have changed, but Christ stays the same,
With joyful hearts, we're glad he came.

CHRISTMAS SNOW

A feeling of Peace envelopes me, I just stretch and yawn.
I lie half awakened, outside the day dawns.
The snowflakes fall so softly; I've no ambition to arise,
My bed feels warm and snugly, and then I realize,
This is Christmas; I can feel it in my soul,
I whisper, "Happy Birthday" to my mom and Jesus,
Outside falls the winter's first snow.

COOMB'S COVE CHOIR

Joy fills your life when you've encountered the Lord
Lifted on wings of eagles and soared
Floating so free with a smile on your face
Blessed and redeemed by immeasurable grace

Doubt flies away like a swallow in flight
Hope floods your soul and gives it new life
Strangers or family it's one and the same
When we gather to worship in the Lord's name

You feel like hugging the whole world tight
When we walk in the presence of that glorious light
Your life is all changed and you really don't care
You've found new peace through friends and prayer

HE'S MY BEST FRIEND

I have a friend so very dear who always understands and cares
He is there when I am happy and when my face is washed with tears.
When my heart is troubled for something wrong I've done,
I cannot find peace of mind until I go before God's Son.

Yes, my best friend is my Saviour and I've often felt His grace
How can He be my friend you ask, if you've not seen His face.
He cannot come to me on earth but His Spirit He does send
And when the Spirit moves on me, I know He's my best friend.

DIALYSIS

I hate to see what you are
going through
Weakness, skin turning a weird
green color
I was so afraid for you and
Cory. I try to leave it in
God's hands but I find it
difficult
When we are at the kidney specialist I can
tell what people are on
dialysis. they have no pink in
their skin and I know their
poor kidneys can't take care
of the poison and toxins building
up in their bodies.
I take a magazine and look at it
I don't want to see the
trials they're going through
and I don't want them to
see the pity in my eyes
If you turned bitter I
would understand. If you
complained I would see why.
I sometimes wish you
would because I would try
to comfort you. Right now
I wish I could do

something, anything to help you
you put on a happy face and
laugh
with everyone you meet.
Cory is getting a new kidney. You
never complained that you
weren't a candidate
you were so proud of John our
son-in-law for giving Cory
his kidney and proud of Cory
for being so brave.
Lester McCarty told me once
that he was glad to be
suffering, because he was
the clay and the potter's
hands were molding him.
So my darling, i think you
have also been made perfect
by the potter's hands
Rest in Peace

NEWFOUNDLAND

The last few premiers of our island,
Boy they've taken quite a stand
Cuts and more cuts, that's what we hear
The brunt of this we cannot bear
No band aids have they passed out yet
To cover up the sore
We've given to the government
We can't give any more

No one here wants to leave
I'm sure I speak for all
But we're forced to leave Newfoundland
To work for a little while
Our focus we have to change
Or things will always be this way
Let's try to stand proud and tall
And help each other today

Why do we buy mussels
From Iceland's waters clear
We have plenty of people
To develop more mussel farms right here
Why is beef imported from New Zealand
I'll never understand
I'm sure we have talent enough
To farm this precious land

Cabbage and beets here grow so well
Berries and rhubarb too
Carrots, onions, cucumbers

We can market our own stew
Let's try it folks you see
We don't have to depend on fish
Create our own meat industry
More poultry, moose, and beef

-2-
Pottery, ceramics, woodworking
Creativity we don't lack
Photographers, painters, musicians
We've just begun to tap
Wine breweries and liquors
We're beginning to understand
We are proud people
Let's develop Newfoundland

Our beauty I have to cover
For no matter where I go
I'll never see more diversity
Rugged cliffs, valleys, and coves
From Port-Aux-Basque's rugged coastline
To St. John's historic past
Golden Sands on the Burin Peninsula
Such beauty will always last

God has given us an island of beauty
A paradise that seldom see strife
An island of different people
Let's make it an island of life
For if we sit in our rocking chairs
Or stand overlooking the bays
We've given up on our children
Please, let's grow stronger today

NEWFIE'S ADVICE TO HIS SOON-TO-BE WIFE

Tatties fried in lard, me love, that's what I really likes
Up on the mainland they add cheese, the crazy little tykes
They call it Au Gratin or something that sounds just grand
But the best way to have tatties is in a frying pan

The frying pan it's got to be hot, if not, it's not the same
Don't fry in Mazola Oil or in no aluminium pan
Just add a little salt, me love, and make em a golden brown
Don't cut em up in no fancy strips but make em nice and round

Don't put them in no darn oven and add no bloody milk
I don't want me old tatties tasting like a piece of silk
And for God's sake, me dear, don't buy no orange coloured yams
Just give me old potatoes fried in the iron pan

Tatties, now, are all dressed up, you add what ever you like
But I don't want no changes made when you become me wife
Me tatties is me greatest love, add em to anything you can
I'll love you even more, me maid, if you fry em in the iron pan

A FRIENDS LAST STORY

I went to visit a dear friend; his life was nearly run,
He talked about his life a bit and some things he had done.
Then he told a story, one I'll not forget,
Of a sister that he had lost, how her last days were spent.

He couldn't be there with her when she departed from this world,
She was only in her twenties, her life not yet unfurled.
He told me how he ran away and hid inside a store,
He couldn't bear to see her suffer or hear her scream once more.

As he told the story the tears ran down his face,
I put my arms around him and tried to give him peace.
Now he is gone to be with God and I know they are together,
Where there are no more tears or pain but love and joy forever.

I never will forget that day, when I sat and talked with Jim.
Sometimes at night I whisper, "God's peace to you my friend."

FOOTSTEPS

When we are young and start to walk,
our footsteps are very slow.
Then we come full circle,
if life permits us to grow old.
Those aging steps
sometimes give us time to set and ponder,
Where we walked along life's road,
and where our footsteps wandered.

Did we run here and there and everywhere,
did we stop to smell the rose?
Did we step in murky mud,
or play with sand between our toes?
Did we focus on pocessions
or concentrate on friends?
Did we stop to give a hug
or take time to make amends?

If God permits us to outlive
our measure of three score and ten,
May we not focus on earthly things;
they're worth nothing in the end.
Let us dwell on friends and family,
forgiveness, joy, and peace.
For in the Heaven that's ours to gain,
those things will never cease.

FORGIVENESS

He was there at our beginning; He'll be there when we die,
Waiting with out-stretched hands to welcome sinners such as I.
We all say things that we regret to our family and our friends,
Father please forgive us and help us make amends.

Wash us with the blood of life and make us lily white,
So we can stand before you and know things are made right.
For even though we believe, sin is always there.
To try and steal Your glory Lord and take us from your care.

Help us Dear Lord every day to draw closer to the truth,
So we can do Your service and help someone here who hurts.
If we can bring someone to You, our lives won't be in vain,
Teach us to look at others needs not for profit or for gain.

We know You love us Dear Lord; Your Spirit we sometimes feel.
How You can love us sinners Lord? It often seems unreal.
Someday we will understand Your loyalty and plans.
Until that time, forgive our sins and hold us in Your hand.

FRIENDS

You have to open up your heart
To have a special friend
Sometimes they say or do things
That you can not comprehend
But you love them for their differences
Though similarity plays a part
You cannot have a true friend
Until you open wide your heart.

GROUP JOURNEY

We are five women on a journey,
On a pathway that will lead to God.
We meet to discuss our joys and failures
As we try to walk the road that Jesus trod.

Like the disciples, we also cling to Jesus,
And rely on the strength of His word.
We ask the Holy Spirit to guide us,
While we try to grow closer to God.

We pray for each heartache and temptation,
Asking God to give us strength to persevere.
In this world where there is so much pain and trouble,
It's good to know, Christ is always near.

Jesus' love is the lifeline we cling to,
The Spirit gives encouragement along the way.
We know our reward will be in Heaven,
Rejoicing with God on that glorious day.

MYSTERIES

There are mysteries in the bible that we don't understand:
Why God sent His Son below to walk this Earth with man,
Why He was born from a Gentile virgin's womb,
Placed in a lowly manger, not in a palace room.

He taught us all to celebrate life; He turned water into wine,
Multiplied bread and fishes so five thousand could all dine.
He walked on stormy waters on the Sea of Galilee.
The greatness of our Savior is one big mystery.

Saul was a sinner but God changed him to Paul,
Restored to him life anew as an example to us all.
He raised Lazarus from the dead; restored sight to the blind.
The ways of God are perfect; there's nothing to refine.

That's why He's our Savior; He also forgives sins,
Makes us proud of who we are and helps us live again.
Someday when we are called to walk those golden stairs,
We'll understand the *mystery* of our Savior who lives there.

HE IS MY CAPTAIN

I'm God's child on this planet called Earth,
I struggle to prove my own worth.
He's my captain and I'll answer His call.
I'll stumble but He won't let me fall.

He carries me over rough sands,
I'm safe in the palm of His hands.
He places me away from the stones,
Where I can walk again on my own.

He's there but He doesn't interfere,
Until I'm in danger or need of His care.
Then He assures me that I'm not alone,
He'll stay with me till I'm safely home.

He's the captain of this universe,
There's no need to hunger or thirst.
I give Him my life and my all,
I'm certain He'll answer my call.

He's my captain on this planet called Earth.
He assures me that I'm really worth,
His blood, His life, and His love,
Until He calls me to His home up above.

THE SHEPHERD CALLS

You say you know Jesus but you don't need prayer
Then you really don't know Jesus.
Are you resting daily in His love and care?
If not, you don't know Jesus.
For the Shepherd calls us every day
To walk with Him and to kneel and pray.
He washed us with the blood of life
Referred to us all the church, His bride.
Yes He calls us every day,
To walk with Him along life's way.
His Spirit He sends to help me through,
He will do the very same for you.
Give to Him every sin and care,
Then you really will know Jesus.

I COUNT ON YOU

Who can I count on Lord? No one but you
You are the only one that I can turn to.
You know my every weakness and trials that I go through,
There's no one else to count on Lord, but I can count on You.

Some nights I lay awake dear Lord and ponder what to do.
All the things that come my way, I see no pathway through.
Without Your hand to guide me, no peace in what I do,
Who can I count on Lord? No one but You.

You keep all my secrets and forgive my every sin,
You wipe away all my tears, so I can smile again.
You make my heart much lighter, thanks for all You do
I find no one to count on Lord, the way I count on You.

Help me Lord to turn to you more often than I do,
Then I wouldn't walk alone as often as I do.
You're the lamp that lights my path and lets me see the truth.
There's no one else to turn to Lord, like I turn to You.

VALENTINE'S DAY

Yesterday, it was paper hearts that we drew ourselves and threw into the porches of our friends. In our town on St. Valentine's Day, we would wait so patiently to see if they'd respond. February fourteenth would come around but no one in our town got teddy bears or tin wrapped hearts to celebrate. We still had lots of fun, as we ran from the houses so no would know and find out who we were.

In preparation, we all would scout the catalogues and then cut things out if something on those pages could be found. We would waste nothing even in our haste to get a valentine to that special one on St. Valentine's Day. We would also make up poems as to each others' homes we'd congregate. I guess the girls more so than boys remember those heart-felt ties that make us think of our homes on St. Valentine's Day.

Those days have all passed away; paper hearts aren't made that way. Big business has taken most of the fun but love is carried on as we celebrate in modern times on St Valentine's Day.

UNCLE BOB'S DOG

This story I tell you and I swear that's it true
about Uncle Bob's dog how through the window he flew.
The night had been cold and the rain turned to ice,
and for poor little Toby it wasn't so nice.

Uncle Bob let his little dog out
to do his buisness without a doubt.
Toby lost his footing and sled down the hill,
went through the window and let out a yelp.

This poor girl was sleeping in on her bed,
with no thoughts of Toby entering her head .
She woke up with a God awful start
with fright enough to accelerate her heart.
Toby, the ice and glass everywhere
it was worse then any scary nightmare.
Uncle Bob was glad that his dog was alright
and sorry that Audrey had a bad fright..

TO BE WITH YOU

I don't want to cross the Jordon, water is my greatest fear,
So, Dear Lord, let me climb those golden stairs.
Is it imagery or dreaming that makes people see those things?
Are there golden roads in Heaven and angels with snowy wings?

Lord, when my time for Heaven comes, I hope that I will see,
A little beam of celestial light as a beacon from you to me.
You said You had to go to prepare a place for us.
Heaven will be beautiful, on your words I'll always trust.

Lord I want to be with You someday, let my troubles fade away
To have that peace that only You can give.
To see again those people that touch us along life's way.
The home You're preparing will be wonderful,
And it's there I want to live.

TOUGH DECISIONS

My unemployment soon runs out,
I don't know what to do.
I might go up to Toronto, to make a buck or two.
Up there me sons, things is so dear,
you can't afford to think.
And they look at you with astonishment,
if you give them a wink.

I can't even open me mouth to speak,
for someone jumps right in.
Did you say you want's a air cut?
What's that suppose to mean?
"Cut off me ear boy," that is what I said.
And they look at me so funny,
I wish that I was dead.

I can't elp it ow I talks,
what's I suppose to do?
Take out a piece of paper,
and write a line or two?
Or perhaps me boy, I should sign,
but Lord I know their minds.
I'd go so fast, they wouldn't keep track,
what solution can I find?

I think I'll stay around ere, me son,
and live on the pokey too.
I can't get through up there I knows,
no matter what I doos.
I'll go to school, I suppose I will.
What do you think?
I got me self in such a state,
I got to ave a drink.

Now I can't sit ere on me arse all day,
I've got to go away.
And when I pass them on the street,
I'll simply say, "Good Day."
And when me air is getting long,
I won't say ear at all.
I'll just go in to them and say,
"for God sakes, shave it all!"

FOOLED UP

I went to the doctor and what did he say
"Fred, I'm sorry, you can die any day."
"Die any day, doctor?" I said.
"Yes, I'm sorry, in a week you'll be dead."
I started walking home and it popped in my head
I should not be walking, I hailed a taxi instead.
When I got home I went straight to the fridge
Pulled out a pie and cut me a wedge.
The doctor's words popped again in my mind
"By not eating right, you lessen your time."
When my wife gets home what will I say?
The doctor said I could die any day.
My tears started falling, I let out a curse
He could not have told me anything worse.
I phoned up my children, invited them in
I greeted them, but my face it was grim.
I broke them the news and everyone said
We won't believe it until you are dead.
That week went faster than ever you could think,
I fixed everything, even the bathroom sink.
The next day I took my dog to the vet,
And while I was there, the doctor I met.
He said, "Fred, old buddy, I've been meaning to call,
The report that I gave you, wasn't yours at all."
I stared at him foolishly and I didn't blink,
I felt like breaking that damn fool's neck.
He scared us all silly, and my wife being so good,
I knew she would kill him if ever she could.
To no more doctors will I go for advice,
For this one has taken ten years off my life.

To all men out there, if it's attention you seek,
You'll get it when doc says, "You'll be dead in a week."
Does loving come because you'll be gone?
Does the wife make up for times she was wrong?
Like faking a headache, or too tired tonight,
But dead in a week makes everything right.

WITHDRAWN

I need to hold you, you're slipping away
Where is the joy of yesterday
I try but you seem not to care
In my heart there's planted a fear
You've withdrawn again from all that's dear

Come back, come back my heart it cries
My brain just echoes, why oh why
Darkness and gloom seem all around
No happiness now can be found
Until at last your smile I see
And the special way you look at me
My heart it jumps with joy again
Free once more from all that pain

You're back from the place I cannot reach
And I realize I soon must teach
Not to retreat when things go black
You know I'll always want you back
Share with me your fears and woe
And only then we can really grow

WE SAW GOD TODAY

I went to church and
I enjoyed it, the hymns, the people.

I thought of Jesus and
how he paid the price for our sins and
I was thankful.

I did not feel his presence nor
did my heart feel unfire for him.

I found Jesus later on that evening, Jonna and
I took some of the blessing bags that
were done to honor her fathers memory.

The first bag was given to an old lady with
barely a tooth in her head, dressed in old rags and
well worn shoes on her feet.

She was so thankful and
she told us that God never lets her down.
All her blessings come from above.

You could see the thankfulness in her eyes.

We felt humbled; this woman with so little thanked and
praised God for what she had been given.
We saw God today.

The Author

Linda Blagdon was born November 25, 1954. She grew up in the small outport of Francois, Newfoundland and currently lives in Windsor, Ontario.

She would like to express her gratitude to all those who have supported her since the publication of this book.

65508722R00045

Made in the USA
Lexington, KY
14 July 2017